In Search

In Search

Becoming who you are...

Ruchi Sharma Kapoor

Anecdote
Publishing House
For the love of quality reading!

Anecdote Publishing House
2nd Floor 2/15 Lane no. 2 Ansari Road,
Daryaganj-110002

Published by Anecdote Publishing House
Copyright © Ruchi Sharma Kapoor

First Edition 2024

ISBN 978-81-968952-1-1

MRP ₹ **299**

All Rights Reserved.
No part of this publication may be reproduced, stored in a retrieval system, or transmitted in any form, or by any means—electronic, mechanical, photocopying, recording or otherwise—without the prior permission of the publisher. Opinions expressed in it are the author's own. The publisher is in no way responsible for these.

Book Promoted and Marketed by Champ Readers Pvt. Ltd.
Edited by Meraki
Cover design by Rishikumar Thakur
Layout by Graphic Tailor
Printed by Thomson Press (India) Ltd, New Delhi

Contents

Prelude   *ix*

The Path   1

Soul Musings   2

One Day…   3

Do you See me?   5

Be Free   7

Be You   8

I am Lost   9

Heart Vs Mind   11

Magic   13

Wanderer   15

You are Awesome   17

You are Seen   19

Why?   22

Those Days	24
Confession	26
Be Kind to Yourself	27
My Story	31
Just	32
Faith	33
You are Enough	35
I am Special	36
Choice	37
I am not Enough	38
Fear	40
The Unknown	41
I am here	42
This or That	44
Fear - My Friend	45
Is there Someone?	48
Don't Know	50
Explore	51
Dealing with Fear	52

Only If…	55
Becoming	56
Fear or Faith	58
The Wild	61
Brave	62
Awareness is the Key	63
Surrender	65
You are not for Everyone	67
Battles	69
Healing	71
Rising Up	73
Progress in a Mess	75
Living from the Heart	77
Some days…	79
The Process	82
Be Curious	84
New Beginnings	86
The Dark	88
Coming Home	91

Stronger than you Think	94
Life and Lessons	97
One Day	99
I am Worthy	100
Close or Far	102
Struggles	105
The Noise	106
Frames	110
My Story	112
Acknowledgements	*115*

To Daddy and Papa
Thank you for always being there for me.
Had it not been for the two of you, search of 'Being Me'
Would never have started.

Prelude

Each one of us is unique and so are our life journeys. No matter who we are, what we do, where we are in our life, we all go through deep struggles and are daunted with questions like, What to do next? Who am I? Do I deserve this? Why is it happening to me? Irrespective of who we are, we all have gone through these and many more. It takes courage to ask the right questions and starting the search for answers is the most important thing one can do in life.

Our entire life we look for answers, we want to be in control of the outcomes, be aware of them.

But it's not the answers that give meaning to our lives, it's the search for answers that gives our life direction and meaning. Even if we don't get the answers, it is important to share and celebrate our journey - the story of our struggles, musings, and desires.

This book is a collection of my musings in my own

search journey of - finding myself, of healing myself and becoming who I am. This book has questions, answers, struggles, and some realizations that I had on the way, that I am sharing here. Read it as you are listening to a friend, it may be your own hidden voice sometimes. You can read it in one go, open it on days when you feel to be heard, read it when you feel nothing is making sense, or just sitting there reminding you 'You got this'.

'In search' is not a destination, it's a continuous journey of being and becoming who you are.

Questions- Simple or complex, or should I call it an 'Itch'. The so called 'Itch' that we all experience at some point of time in our lives, it has nothing to do with age, role or a situation. The itch that comes in form of unhappiness, that feeling that something is missing, like we are doing everything wrong, having it all, yet looking for something more….

This is the time when life is pushing us to make some choices. Not easy ones at all, the ones that really need all our inner strength and conviction. A support, a comforting hand would have been good, but no one tells us, this journey is ours and we have to walk alone….

The biggest pain is the feeling of 'I don't exist'. It is toughest to go unnoticed by the people you love. It feels as if we don't matter at all, the hurt and pain that comes along…but when the path is ours, there will be a supreme power always surrounding us with what we need.

Walking alone with all our fears, doubts, pain, and confusion…and finding something on the way.

What is the struggle for?
Is it for survival, acceptance, excellence, love, winning,
or being right?
The quest so strong, yet so ambiguous
Wonder how it is holding us all?

The Path

The path will be tough and lonely

Each day you will have to brace yourself

There will be days when you will feel burnt out

Days when you will feel left out

Days when you will question yourself

Don't look back, don't falter

Brace yourself and keep walking

Have faith and keep walking

Just remember, one day it will all make sense

Soul Musings

Sitting in a silent corner of the room, looking for peace

The noise inside makes it impossible to feel

I look away, close my eyes, try to silence the mind

The pain doesn't go away, the sinking feeling forces me to seek help & mercy from the unknown

The sun stops to shine and the night is prolonged

Darkness seems to be the only friend that I am left with

All this is part of the plan and there must be a reason

What unsettles the mind often gives solace to the soul

For finally it is on its journey way back home.

One Day...

One day, it all makes sense – yes, it does!

The people you meet, the mistakes you make, the decisions you take,

It all makes sense

Doesn't matter how many times you cried,

Were left hurt or lost,

What matters is how many times you stood up and how?

Because in the end it will all make sense

Remember the day when you were all alone, hoping for someone to be with

How angry and rejected you felt?

Just so you know, it's all for a reason and in the end, it'll all make sense

Times when there was no energy and you didn't feel like fighting anymore

In Search: Becoming who you are...

Days when you almost gave up on yourself and life still flowed

Because someone up there knows – in the end it will all make sense

When life is harsh and shows you no sign of mercy

When living itself looks meaningless and blurry

Brace yourself, be kind and keep walking

In the end it will all make sense!!

Do you See me?

I do get moved, when you see through me

I feel a little shaken, when I find myself alone

I do doubt myself, when success is not coming my way

I do feel deprived when no encouragement comes my way

Shattered, broken, I close my eyes and fall to the ground

But don't think this is the end

My story doesn't end here, like phoenix, I shall rise

With my faith, I shall soar high

For I have learnt to stand tall with my broken pieces

I don't get defined by what others think of me

The days you feel lonely and beaten, hold yourself tight and be kind. This is the relation you can't fail in.

Pick up your broken pieces and start again with love. This is not a formula for victory but recipe for 'Compassion'.

If I were to get you at the cost of being me- I don't want you!

Be Free

Don't hold yourself back, because they can't handle you

They have tried enough, to pull you down

You're too aggressive, weak, emotional, sensitive, impractical…

These and beyond are just bars to cage your spirit

For years you have lived within these bars

Set yourself free and SHINE

For you have it all

Don't exhaust yourself, to prove them

Let your shine blind them

Because you are the power – in you the Universe resides

Let there be no other way

Than, just being YOU

Be You

Be who you were born to be

Take your time and live your journey that takes you 'Home'

There will be pit stops – don't get confused with them and settle for anything less

Because you may like it there – but your soul will be unsettled

This is not philosophy or some idealistic concept

This is about you and me

Be who you were born to be

I am Lost

You can't hear me

Probably I can't hear myself too

The chaos inside is confusing

How can I get lost on my own path?

Is it the fear of the destination or the pain of walking alone?

I am not sure if this is the pain

Or a strange numbness of being isolated, a feeling that I am being left alone?

It's a strange place to be in – I see everyone fading away and no one noticing me

Like air will I vanish from here and from people's heart?

Like a star I will shine with all my warmth

My words will then begin to make sense

It's there in your isolated bubble we will meet again

For I will always hold you, my friend

Heart Vs Mind

It's tough to express yourself

It's tougher to know what to express?

Humans are God's most amazing creation

Human brain with experience has power to silence the heart

Silenced enough – It's strange how still our heart always knows the answer

Mind often celebrates its victory over heart

These celebrations then feel hollow and the heart then wanders

Every argument is not for you to win, some should be left to time to respond.

'Don't be scared of the dark or the unknown path
Lean in and meet your strongest self'.

'If you were to scream for attention, scream it to yourself. If you were to beg for love, love yourself. If you were to look for validation, seek validation within'.
'Asking these from others is like getting drenched in rain, waiting for an umbrella - when you can just walk inside the home'.

'You are happy, when others are happy.
You are happy, when 'YOU' are happy.
The first hypothesis, however, is still to be validated'.

Magic

When life becomes dull or our spirits are low – there are always those who just know

Like magic, they show up, in one of their own special ways

With their warm smile, hug, our favourite food, drink or just with their presence

They stand by us in thick and thin of life

Reducing our pain in difficult times and multiplying our joys in celebrations

This 'Magic Circle' is our family and friends who add colours to our lives

The 'Magic Circle' needs to be thanked and celebrated for what they mean to us

Make time and go all out and create those warm and nurturing memories with family and friends because as they say 'When we have each other, we have everything'.

Life is too short to be just lived focussed on the 'Should's'.

Make each day beautiful, spend time with loved ones, make memories.

Because one day we all will go, the memories have the power to hold you when you have nothing. Make them special.

Wanderer

I wander and wonder about life – the biggest mystery of all times

There is darkness and, in that darkness, lurks hope

There are many questions with few answers

Questions with no answers are powerful & beautiful too

There is a mind unsure of its existence

The same mind is courageous enough to move mountains and dive into deep oceans

There are diligent prayers, always asking for more

Carelessly overlooking what have already been bestowed

The heart has enough warmth to heal the world

Still, it aches for connection and acceptance from a few people

There is a lot of struggle and loneliness

In Search: Becoming who you are...

And it's this struggle that gives birth to the strongest self

'One Day' is eagerly awaited to be celebrated

When, every day can be that day

Everyone is in a hurry to reach somewhere, to achieve something

When all we ever need has always been with us

I wander and wonder about life - the biggest mystery of all times

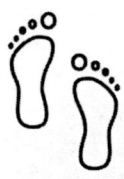

You are Awesome

Whether you like to talk or stay quiet

Whether you like to share your troubles or keep them tight

Whether you like to sing along or hymn when you are alone

Whether emotions flow easily to you or there is a struggle to express

Whether you reach out for help or your problems are just your own

Whether you can express love easily or feel loved is to be understood

Whether you forgive easily or it's difficult to let go

Whether you steadily dance to all tunes of life or topple over the rocky music

Whether you face all storms head on or hide till it settles down

In Search: Becoming who you are...

Whether you take risks fearlessly or each step is guided

It doesn't matter

This is who you are, and you are AWESOME – Remember that!!

You are Seen

I see you are struggling and on the verge of giving up

I want to tell you; this is just a phase and shall pass

I see, you were hopeful things will be ok, but it's just getting worse day by day

Things are falling one by one

I want to tell you; you are doing great and your efforts will not go waste

I see despite trying so hard, giving in all you have, things are not working out

It's like a tunnel with no end and you are alone in the dark

It's so lonely out here, all you wish is someone who can hold you

I want to tell you, you are not alone, there is someone always watching over you and will not let you fall

In Search: Becoming who you are...

I see the weight of your own thoughts wears you out

All your body and mind crave for is some peace and time-out

I want to tell you, listen to your body, go easy on yourself

You are well deserving of some rest.

I see nothing seems to make a difference, things and people have lost their charm.

You feel you are failing and not enough to be managing it well.

I want to tell you, you are an amazing person, and you are doing just fine.

You are ENOUGH as you are and LOVED for who you are.

Every adversity in life makes you stronger and not immune. Don't confuse being strong with not being impacted with anything. Being strong means being resilient and being resilient does not mean being insensitive.

It doesn't matter how much others agree with your way of living.
What matters is are you at peace with your way of living?

It's not about proving someone wrong; it is not about being respectful to someone, it is about YOU. It's about how your deepest self want to be seen.
You fight, struggle, feel discontented or isolated when somewhere you doubt yourself.
Trust yourself- you are all you have.

Till we reach our final frame, choose not to be caged by any frame.

Right or Wrong are like colours in the sky,
depends on what time of the day it is, and which direction you are looking at.

Why?

I often ask 'Why am I here?'

There has to be a reason for my existence

A reason bigger than just meeting daily needs

This itch to find yourself, starts with a struggle

The struggle which tells you what you are doing is not right, is not what you need to do

The surety gives you the courage to take the leap of faith – walking the unknown path.

There is different calmness here,

No hurry to reach anywhere, just a deep desire to find myself

The question still remains – why am I here? Why was I chosen?

No answer yet

All I am sure, there is a reason

If only I am able to find it or it will find me

Is this what they call the search for purpose?

Will I ever get to experience what it is like to reach the destination, the final one?

Till I find out, I enjoy this journey, this is challenging, making me stronger

It's taking me away and yet getting me closer

And just being here, I know there is a reason

Those Days

There will be days you will be down in the dumps

When you don't want to give up; but have no strength to stand up and go through it once again

Lying face down you are probably thinking all the times you have stood back and asked – why can't things be ever ok for me?

Is it too much to ask for? Am I asking too much from life?

Lying still with your head down, close your eyes and almost deciding to quit

From the corner of your eye you see that one person, who is eagerly waiting for you to get back

You don't realise but you are someone's hope and inspiration

And in that moment, you will get back up

If you don't understand someone's struggle, dreams, despair, don't be quick to judge them as weak or weird.
People are different my dear, Universe has different paths for all.
Someone's truth isn't prettier just because it's a reality.
Everyone's truth comes alive at its own time.
If you can, partner with someone to witness their truth coming alive.
Hold the space with kindness and compassion, make way for something new to be created and seen.

Confession

I can understand it's difficult for you to understand me all the time.

I am aware that I leave you confused sometimes

The reason I say this with so much conviction is – I don't always get myself too

I am struggling but I am healing and that's true

At times I just go with the flow and meet a side of me I have never realised existed before

I am so sure about something and I go ahead and do it, only to realise that it was a mistake

I am not mad, crazy, I am not running away either

I am rebuilding myself to be with you forever

Be Kind to yourself

It's ok to make mistakes sometimes

Just that don't make them your reasons to discard yourself

It's ok to be fearful at times, just that it should not become your barrier to move

It's ok wanting to be alone at times, just that it should not become your mechanism to stay away from people

It's ok to get defeated, just that let it not shake your confidence to try again

It's ok to be heartbroken sometimes, just that don't restrict love forever

It's ok to fall sometimes, just don't choose to walk with crutches always

It's ok to just breathe at times and let go off things, just that don't make it your way of surviving

It's not easy to stand still in this fast-moving world. Where everyone around you is chasing something - money, fame, power, security... .

Standing firm on your ground with faith requires courage and to be brave.

This is a superpower - brace it, for not all are blessed with it. Because it is a superpower.

I fail so many times, but my failures don't define me. I am a work in progress, and if no one else, I will stand with myself and hold myself gently.

Sometimes it's critical to be the person and behave with yourself the way you expect someone else to do.

We all know the pain of going unseen, not being enough.

Lives are wasted in waiting to just hear 'I am proud of you', 'I acknowledge your struggle and I see you', 'I love you for who you are.'

Emotionally unavailable parents, harsh society, judgemental friends, critical partners... .

But, above all these, we have ghosted ourselves the most.

We give ourselves the toughest times.

We are the only thing we got and yet our inner voice is filled with harsh words for us.

We wait for others, who by no means are in our control, to say nice things to us. And we ourselves, choose to speak in a manner doubting our own existence.

'I am a looser', 'I am worthless', these words have haunted so many of us.

One favour we need to do to ourselves more than anyone else - Be Kind.

We all seem to have gotten it all wrong.
We are exhausting ourselves searching... God knows what?
How many more moments will we lose before we realise the race is pointless,
It's here in the moment that we have it all.
As we realise this 'Magic unfolds'.

My Story

I love my story

Not sure if it's beginning or the end

But I love my story

I am neither the hero, nor the victim or the villain

I am the author of my story

I write new chapters – there is pain and there is failure

There is laughter and there is connection

There is joy and there is celebration of LIFE!!

Just

Just because my choices don't fit the race

Just because I don't live to chase

Just because I prefer to get drenched in the rain

Just because I cry when in pain

Just because I follow my heart

Just because I choose to make my own path

Just because I often fail

Just because I honour my emotions

Just because fame, power doesn't excite me

Just because I think from my heart

Just because I easily own up my part

I am not a loser

I am just different and special.

Faith

Today I may not have the answers

Today I might look weak and stupid

Today I am lost

But I am still walking

For I have faith in my angel

I have faith when I fall

My angel gives me courage to again stand tall

I have faith when I cry

My angel watches me over and wipes my tear before they dry

I have faith when I lose my path

My angel will pull me back

In Search: Becoming who you are...

I have faith, I have a calling, the reason for me being alive

I have faith I am being directed to something, becoming who I am in the process.

You are Enough

No matter what get accomplished and what is left undone

With all the accolades and feedback that may come

I want you to know – you are enough as you are

With days when you feel you could have done better

Days when you felt you were on top

I just want you to know you are enough as you are

When grumpiness is all over your face and you just don't want to talk

You probably want to sit and take a life stalk

Do know – its ok and you are enough as you are

You are enough for people to love you with all their heart

You are the hope that keeps your family warm

You are the strength that keeps them going

You are enough as you are

I am Special

I am special, I just know it

Not because for what I have accomplished or done

But the way I honour my emotions, I am special

Not because I have never done anything wrong

But because I have always stood back strong – I am special

Not because I have an extraordinary story

But because I am willing to tell my story – I am special

Not because I don't fall

But because I don't pretend to have it all – I am special

Not because I never feel lonely

But because I love deeply – I am special

Not because I have a lot of relationships

But because I nurture the ones I have – I am special

Choice

I have today with me

I have a choice - do I want to live it regretting about the past ?

Or

Live planning it for tomorrow?

Or

Choose to live today and give my best?

I choose to laugh a little more,

Play a little more,

Celebrate a little more and

Be 'me' a little more

To be away from all negative emotions and judgements

To just 'BE'

I am not Enough

I am not enough; stems from I have not thought enough

Not thought enough: how unique and special I am?

What I bring to people around me?

What do I feel and think?

It's not about telling these to others, it's about knowing these about yourself

Being enough is feeling enough as you are.

Fear

Meet my buddy - someone with whom I have spent most of my time. I would be petrified of it and it has turned my life upside down on many occasions, but now I know it's a friend. For it has taught me resilience, how to experience joy, and live life to the fullest. Got me closest to myself.

We all have been there - reasons differ but we all have been there. Fear of being abandoned, fear of losing, fear of not being good enough, fear of something going wrong , fear of the unknown.

How we wish we are rescued, there is someone who understands us and offers a solution.

Irrespective of our association with this emotion, it is seen as an unwanted guest. The pain that comes with it is immense but only if we let it pass it's life changing. It is through this pain the new chapters of life are written, for now we realise, we are the one writing these and not the ones just playing the part.

Fear is inevitable, no matter what we do, how strong we become it will be there. It is telling us there are still some parts those needs to be heard and healed.

Fear

Let not others cash on our fears

Let not our fears make way for others to take advantage of us

Fear of being judged,

Fear of not being good enough,

Fear of being laughed at

Fear of being alone

Our fears don't make us weak; they are an indication that an area still needs to be healed

Our fears are an opportunity to be a stronger version of self

'Our actions should be an outcome of possibilities that it will create and not our fears'.

The Unknown

Scared, staring into the unknown

There is too much at risk, to be able to let go

Don't have it in me to go through the drill once more

Leaning in all the faith that I know

Resistance walks shouldering with all my faith

I am wondering if I have learnt the right lesson in the past?

I will walk in the unknown with trembling feet and a heart full of prayers for support and help

And then I will be held through whatever it is

I have done this dance before; all I always remember is taking the first trembling step into the unknown and rest is Faith

I am Here

If only you can see me, you can understand me

I have been talking to you, like staring in the dark

Doubting only myself, of not speaking loud enough

Took me time to understand

It's not me, it's you, who can't see me or hear me

I had to just look the other side, to the light, to be seen and heard.

It's not easy to love yourself, especially on days, when you struggle to understand your reason for existence.
Not easy to hold yourself, when your existence looks meaningless.
Tough when everything around you is moving fast and you are still.
This is the time for self-love
Self-love isn't always about pampering yourself, not about feeling proud of yourself; it's also about 'Just being' and being ok with it.

Our silence is precious
Not everyone can understand it
One needs to be able to sit with us, through our struggle, through pain, through mystery...and then one will know how our silence speaks.

This or That

We can't have it all, were never supposed to have it all anyways

That's not the design

Life is a journey of exploring choices,

And choices are about THIS or THAT

Every moment we make a choice, and with every choice we have the ability to shape up our lives the way we want them to

There are no good or bad choices, they are just in a moment choice

One choice doesn't make or break us, unless we stop believing we have choices

Choice is power and it's for you to make

The more you lose yourself with every choice, the more helpless you feel

Fear – My Friend

I am in a long-committed relationship with 'Fear'

Fear – of losing something, fear of something going wrong

For reasons unknown it comes slowly from nowhere

And the moment it shows up, my entire life is hijacked by it

I know it all too well

He is one who stands absolutely next to me, shoulder to shoulder

It is so close, that I can't feel anyone or anything else near me

I talk a lot to it

I ask if I did some mistake for it to show up again?

Like a lost friend I ask 'How come you are here today'?

In Search: Becoming who you are...

I tried becoming friends with it, so many days we spend with just us

No matter how much I hate it, it teaches me something every time it comes

And comes back again and again, not sure how much more there is to learn

Every time it goes, I feel that now I have learnt, and now I am free

And just then, from somewhere far I can hear it coming back again

At times life gets so tough living with fear, feel like I don't deserve to be alive

I beg, I get angry, I plead, I apologise - I have done everything for it to disappear

But never gave up, never stopped.

This fear didn't let me give up,

When I am up the whole night sitting with my fear, still the next morning I am there welcoming the new day

Every part of my body and mind is exhausted fighting with fear, I still show up for my loved ones

When I am broken from inside and just pleading for it

to end, still I am trying to make someone smile

It tells me 'I am stronger than I think'

Fear is my friend; it strengthens my Faith

Is There Someone?

I am so confused

Wish someone could just come and show me the way

It's not easy, when your heart and mind are in conflict, like running on parallel tracks.

Is it really my mind? Or collective mind of people around me?

There is a cacophony happening inside me

Having so much at stake is not making the matter any easier.

I believe the answer lies within me

What if I can't hear it, what if I don't want to?

What if the collective minds say it's wrong? They are stronger in number than my mind.

My happiness is what I want

Why does it sound selfish to the collective minds? Isn't it what we all are chasing in our own ways?

To me it is liberating

Why doesn't my idea fit the world frame?

Question is,

Does it have to?

Don't Know

I don't know what I am doing is right or wrong?

But I know you know

And your knowing is more important than mine

Because you are the one guiding me, in a direction I didn't think I could ever walk

I can't look ahead into the future, never could

I can take the next step, following your instruction

That's what I am doing, and look how far I have come

I have walked along with fear, it has exhausted me

Fear is real and so is faith

Where fear ends, faith begins or it's the other way round?

Let faith take me forward... .

Explore

Away from the world outside, towards a world inside me,

There is abundance, and there is unconditional love,

I like being here, for here I crave for nothing, I fear nothing,

I don't have to prove anything, or long for acceptance….

This is the real home.

Where world outside hurts, this 'home' heals.

Dealing with Fear

Two cliffs facing each other with a deep valley connecting the two

If I have no choice but to jump off from one to the other

Scary as hell

I am not the kind who will start thinking of ways to do it smartly, as to minimize the hurt

Or start practicing my long jumps to ensure my best shot

I have huge respect for people who can do it, I am not one of them

I am scared, petrified, in deep pain because of all the fear surrounding with thoughts of what will happen when I fall…

I freeze, stand like a stone, no energy to move at all….

Then with trembling feet, I start to walk towards the

edge

On my way, I go silent, knowing there is no way out and I have to face this, let go off everything, every attachment, every resentment, viewing my life all over again, surprisingly have new realisations, being grateful for what I have

Complete surrender

I reach the edge almost in trance, I don't look at the cliff ahead neither at the valley in between

Taking one last deep breath, I do what needs to be done

I don't jump, I take my first step into the blank and

I am held

What are you lost with?
Are you lost with being busy?
OR
Lost with finding self?
Lost being busy – takes you away from reality
Finding self makes you the reality

The journey to find self is beautiful and mysterious
Once you start, even when the end looks far, or the journey is difficult, you can't go back
You may feel lost, stagnant- as if you are not moving ahead.

Being static is a movement too, because that's when you are going deeper with self.

Only If...

If only you can see me, you will understand me

I have been talking to you, doubting only myself…

Maybe I am not being loud enough, maybe I chose a wrong time….

Took me a while to understand

It's not me, it's you

You are unable to hear me, because you don't see me…

I had to just shift my focus, look the other side

Saw the light, was seen and heard

Becoming

Becoming who you are one step at a time

I am more aligned to the word 'becoming' than 'become'

Becoming….

A work in progress, still unsure of the final outcome

Not sure how does it look like

A confirmed outcome is a myth, it's a cage, that keeps us away from fully exploring the mystery

If I decide what I want to be, how do I be sure this is what I had to be?

It's not bad to have a goal, just unfair for us to be its slaves

Sometimes life takes its own course and we need to trust it and be willing to go with it

Being on a growth path means you will falter often,
be aware of the same. This awareness will get you
back to your path.

Having all the answers can be tricky.
Some of the greatest discoveries start with 'I don't
know'.

It's easy to get angry,
But difficult to understand 'WHY'.

Loneliness is not about no one understands me.
It's either.
You not sharing what is important to you
OR
You only sharing what is important to you.

People are busy finding themselves at the wrong
addresses.

Fear or Faith

Fear and Faith are inversely proportional

I have a deep relation with 'Fear'

It's a friend that visits me often and when it shows up, I get sucked by it completely

I start living from my head, like nothing around me exists

It takes a lot of strength to move through daily tasks in such a situation, it's an act of sheer braveness and courage

But this is the place where my connection with God, my angels, the Universe becomes the strongest

The connection that liberates me like a free soul, making me lighter

This is such a gratifying experience; I often wonder why can't I move directly to this?

Not sure if that's possible, or I haven't been able to discover it yet

I am an emotional being,
I feel deeply - I cry often, I smile fully, I get hurt, I get upset...

These emotions exist because I am human
They clear the way for me to be strong
They don't break me down; they build me up

The Wild

Amidst a dense forest, there is fast moving road, cutting the forest equally into two

The forest is dense and looks scary

For who may be courageous and curious enough to step into it, leaving the safe, fast-moving road

People daring to step out of into the wilderness, are seen as wrong and stupid by the people on the road

Once you step into the wilderness, what looks scary earlier, provides, peace and joy

Once here you look at your fellow beings compassionately and say a silent prayer for them

May you soon realise, the road has no end, and what you are chasing, lies within you in the wilderness.

Brave

I wanted to be seen as 'Brave'

Tried very hard, pretended a lot, tried to prove myself

And then, somewhere on the way got very tired

I accepted, I am not 'Brave' and stopped fighting the futile battle

Somewhere on the journey I realised, I was judging myself against the definition of being Brave, that has been drilled into me

That didn't feel right, it looked like a privilege to a few and to my mind there are more brave people out there

I decided to come up with my own definition

Ability to show up as you are – funny, boring, irritating, motivational, sorted, confused…

I am 'Brave', because I am me

Awareness is the Key

Be aware enough of things that derail you

Be courageous enough of letting go off the derailers

Be brave enough to listen to your heart

Be kind enough to take care of yourself

Be creative enough to do something that makes you feel alive

Be daring enough to show up as you are

Be authentic enough to speak what you want to say

Be confident enough to not fear failure

Be human enough to feel and heal.

The desire to be one with the 'who I am,' is the
biggest mystery and the ultimate journey.
You don't abandon yourself for this,
You embrace yourself,
Don't be attached to anything and be found,
Being here, yet not in here.

Surrender

At times we just freeze in our place

Choosing not to do anything and hoping for this time to pass

We don't take charge of the situation and kind of give up

We just don't have it in us to go through it

We live every moment in fear, anxiety, helplessness…

We become ok to face anything & everything, and wish the unknown just comes, because we can't hold it anymore

But, that's not the design

This time will not pass, till we go through it feeling every bit of the discomfort

The moment doesn't ask for us to give up,

It's here to teach us 'Surrender'

In Search: Becoming who you are...

To do what we got to do, with no strings attached to the outcome

Breathe through it with 'Faith', whatever will happen will be a part of our story

It will be a part that will take us closer to home

You are not for Everyone

Not everyone can understand you

Not everyone would see the person you are

Not everyone would appreciate you for who you are

All of this hurts, it will ache your heart

Pause for a while and feel the pain

Cry if you want to

But don't stop being you and doing what you got to do.

'The fear of being judged has held more captives than what all wars put together would have ever had
You are all you have - nurture and be kind'.

Battles

So many battles are fought, some visible and many invisible

The battles don't necessarily have a winner or a loser

Some battles end in surrender and acceptance

The battles fought inside are draining

We all have fought a lot of battles, most of them are unknown to the world

Life is a teacher; it has its unique ways of teaching

We don't have to pass or fail, only learn and move on

The lessons keep repeating in different forms or shape, till we learn

Lessons are not easy always, but are totally worth it

The more I stop avoiding myself and accept myself,
the less friction I feel with others.

'Dear Fear – my friend from a long time. You are here
to teach me something. Thank you.
But can you please be a little kind, I will learn. Please
be kind to me'.

Healing

Blessed are those who realise they need healing

Healing from the past, from the grudges, un-attended emotions, self-doubt, arrogance, fear, insecurity….

We have quite a few heads walking around, wanting to change the world, but blinded to what in them needs a change

No wonder we live in a disconnected world, dealing with loneliness as our top concern

Some crossroads in life are just special.

You don't choose which way to go, you are kind of chosen…

And then you are never the same person again, something in you changes forever…

Rising Up

There are days when life is happening outside of you

Everything is moving, happening as it is supposed to

But you are far away, in something like a deep pit, all by yourself

Trying to figure out what is happening?

Your mind knows, there is nothing in here, you have to get out

But still, you continue to be there and watch

Watch how you are all by yourself, how dark and lonely it's there, watch how everything is moving so fast….

There is something unique about this sitting and watching

There is no panic, no fear, no resistance, you are not trying to get out of here,

Like you have made peace with the place

In Search: Becoming who you are...

Deep inside you know this place isn't right, because you can't feel anything, you don't feel you are alive

Then one day, not sure how,

The world starts to come closer; you can see and feel a little

But how is this happening?

You are very sure you haven't moved…then what is it that is getting things closer to you?

The ground beneath you starting to rise, taking you closer to life

When the resistance stops and there is acceptance; magical things happen

This is the design, and this is the path.

Progress in a Mess

I am messed up, yes, I am, in more ways than one

I can very well feel this mess, but don't know how to address that

Where to start, how to start?

Not even sure how I got so far?

After all, was I doing that bad?

But now I am here, where to now?

It would have been nice to get some help in picking me up

Someone dusting the mud off me

But there is just me.

I again ask myself – what now?

What do I want?

And the blank stare is the only response

In Search: Becoming who you are...

Not being sure of what you want is a blessing sometimes

Since, whatever I do will be a movement from where I am

There won't be any benchmarks to measure my success against

Any and every movement will be success

That thought is relieving, gives me a faint smile

The mess, however dirty, deep it is, somehow doesn't look hopeless anymore

For nothing else, but my mind has moved from where it was stuck

And I can tell you progress has been made and the process has begun.

Living from the Heart

In this world of overachievers, we are outliers

In a world where everyone is moving so fast, chasing something

We are just surviving, not wanting anything

In this journey called life, everyone gets tired at some point of time

Tired of constantly trying to achieve and prove something, tired of aimlessly chasing something, tired of faking and pleasing people, tired of neglecting yourself....

At that juncture you question the relevance of everything you have done so far

The very way of living your life looks flawed

The right and wrongs, the ego fights, the struggle to be accepted

Nothing seems to matter now and we wonder what was the point of it all

In Search: Becoming who you are...

Your entire life runs in front of your eyes, and you are left staring at it in despair of why didn't I live?

In those moments what will hold us and keep us from breaking down is the love and warmth in our heart.

Some Days...

Some days, with my words I can motivate an entire army

Some days, an entire army is not enough to pull me out of my bed

Some days, I have the energy to move mountains

Some days, lifting my own hand is impossible

Some days, I understand & appreciate the deepest life lessons

Some days, I question my own existence

Some days, my heart is filled with so much warmth, love and kindness

Some days, my heart feels so deprived of love that I feel lonely

I wonder which one of this is 'Me'?

I think and think some more....

In Search: Becoming who you are...

All these days and many more are all 'Me', each of them reflects a part of 'Me'

I don't regret any of these versions

In fact, I smile; my heart filled with gratitude

For I have lived fully through each of these days; felt the pain and the joy

This whole self is 'Me' and I cherish each part of me.

I am the home I have been looking for!

When there is no fear to miss a destination or a goal the journey becomes beautiful and joyful.

The Process

When you are on your journey, a journey that you are creating with each step. It gets difficult to explain it to others, others who are still guided by pre-set parameters

Sometimes simple questions like 'What is happening?' can send you on an awkward spiral. Without realising, you start answering, justifying yourself with some facts and some cover ups

Each of such conversation will leave you feeling strained and wondering 'Why'?

It's ok!

Don't worry

Most of the people asking questions to you are not really interested in knowing what is happening with you

Your inward spiral is an outcome of your own vulnerability of proving your self-worth with criterion engrained in our belief system

Be Kind to yourself, give yourself time, trust the process and you will be fine.

Be Curious

In case wondering with what?

Start with self

Be curious towards self

Being curious with ourselves is the first step towards living a joyful life.

When a storm strikes, when we struggle to see light

We are scared and wait for things to settle right

So that we can walk ourselves back home

What no one tells is, there is no going back

We don't move back to, we move towards

That is our Home.

The greatest role that we can play in this life is of being a
'Conscious Traveller'.

New Beginnings

What is happening here?

I am not fearful anymore and can't feel any excitement too

I don't get angry now but unable to love fully

I am not getting hurt anymore but am not feeling happy either

What is it that I am doing wrong here?

I have tried to be strong to be able to protect myself

I have stood for myself not needing anything from anyone

And I have been able to do that, I should have felt joyful

But where has the joy gone?

I have not become strong; I have become closed

All emotions originate from the heart, But I have closed the gates

Keeping all at bay.

Life has its own plans - when we seem to have got a hang of things and sailing through life calmly, we get off tracked to a dark and bumpy road.

It keeps getting darker, messier, scarier……. lonely.

We struggle because this is new.

Why have we landed here? What is coming now? Till when we will be here?

Is there some help coming our way?

Lot of questions and no answers, just realisation after realisation..

We are not off-tracked.

We are moving towards a new destination, a different destination than what we had thought.

As we move along, we realise it's not always us who choose our journeys, some journeys just chose us.

We are the chosen one.

The Dark

I am here, I am lost, I am stuck

I am here, somewhere, amidst the clouds…

Not sure whether I am being led somewhere or just standing firm on my ground

How long has it been?

Life is about movement, then why I am stuck here?

Why am I alone here? Are there others as well, who are stuck in this place, would I know them?

Will these clouds ever fade away?

I want to see, I want to feel where I am, how far have I come?

I hope I have covered some distance, was not an easy journey at all

I had to let go off a lot of things

I vaguely remember when this all started, I had not planned for it

These clouds are getting intense, they are tiring me, what if I give up?

What will giving up look like?

So many questions, and no answers?

I am here, somewhere, I am lost…waiting to be found.

I may not know what exactly is happening with me right now?
I may not know when this all started and till when it will continue
What I do know is, I am no longer the same person who walked into this,
And
I will not be the same person who walks out of it.

Coming Home

The journey of coming home starts differently for everyone

Its route is unique for each one of us

Sometimes it looks like healing

Sometimes it's suffering

Sometimes it's pain

Sometimes it's immense happiness

Sometimes it's being alone

The journey is different and not linear

There will be days we feel we are on a right track, we've got this, and just then you will be face down in an unknown path

Suddenly the storms that you thought you have left behind,

Covers you all over again

In Search: Becoming who you are...

You are sucked once again into the darkness wondering what did I do wrong?

Alas, after bearing all the pain and suffering from my past, I was walking on a steady path

Why again?

I will have to start from scratch? I don't think I have it in me to walk the path again

While in the darkness with your eyes closed, face covered in mud & dirt

You will realise, this storm is not the same, it's different, because you are not the same person who started the journey

You are down and broken right now, but there is light inside you. The light that you created while withering the earlier storms

However bleak, and tiny that light may be, you have it within you

Be aware about this, and you will know you can do this.

For understanding me, you don't have to feel what I am feeling
Please know this, that's not what I mean when I say -
I want to be understood
To be understood is; listening to me and allowing me to feel what I am feeling in the moment, without any judgement

My self-worth is not dependent on what I do
It's who I am, what I think, how I show up.

Love deeply with your whole heart
The ability to love deeply, it's the boat that keeps us afloat during stormy nights.

Stronger than you Think

You are Stronger than you think

You may choose to see yourself as a nobody, but you are the strength for someone.

You may choose to see yourself as a weak person, but you are the one who has stood back post a fall, every single time.

You may choose to see yourself as unworthy of love, but you are the one who spreads smiles effortlessly to others.

You may choose to see yourself as someone incapable of managing tough situations, but you are the one who has withered many stormy nights all by yourself.

You may be scared of being left unseen, unloved, but you are the one whose kindness knows no boundaries.

Don't pull yourself down, by fearing the unknown.

Challenges will come, things will get messy, remember, you are stronger than you think.

You have stood alone by yourself when surviving looked impossible.

You have spread joy and kindness to others when you were broken inside.

You have stood back from all the face down moments.

You are strong, kind and worthy.

The day I stopped seeing people as villains and myself as a victim of circumstances, I discovered something beautiful and powerful – ME.

Sometimes the only answer is 'Acceptance'.
Acceptance means not to ask 'Why me?'
'When will it end?', 'Who is responsible for this?'
Acceptance means – 'What is it teaching me?' 'What more inner work needs to be done?' and have faith.

Life and Lessons

They say life gives us lessons.

Yes, it does.

But how many are they?

Do we ever get to a point when we have learnt it all?

I don't think so, at least I am far from that point.

They say life repeats its lessons till we learn it well.

What does learning well means?

Does it mean life has a grading pattern?

Does it mean we now have the answers and are fully prepared to face the same lesson?

I don't think so.

Life lessons evolve us as individuals, our perspectives, our thoughts, our reactions.

They come to our rescue in multiple situations and not

just restricted to the said lesson.

Life is not interested in grading us

Sometimes the lessons will never repeat they are precursors to something we may need in the future

Life doesn't want us to be robots, to not get impacted by anything.

It just wants to cushion us, create the warmth within when we are cold.

We have to stop looking at life like an exam….

It's a journey and every moment is an experience.

One Day

And one day, just like that, it will all make sense.

It will all make sense, giving answers to all your doubts, all mysteries will fall in place.

The journey till 'That Day' however is not dark and gloomy; it's painful and lonely.

To all those who are in the journey, I want to tell, 'Your struggle is real, I see you.'

'I see your scars and how you embrace them, sometimes with tears and sometimes with armour.'

This is all for a reason, the reason much bigger than you can ever imagine, you are the chosen one.

Remember you don't choose such journeys; some journeys just choose you.

Keep walking, taking one breath at a time and one day, just like that it will all make sense.

I am Worthy

There is so much to do,

Tasks to be completed, planning to be done.

And, here I am, giving myself all the time to do nothing.

I am giving myself time to be ready.

One look at the open items, tasks left incomplete, I start feeling anxious and guilty.

Then I gently remind myself

'I am the most important task, and I am worthy of this rest.'

The list keeps getting bigger and expectations soaring higher.

On loop are the questions, 'When, how long and why?'

Self-doubt starts to creep in, is it just a cheap tactic for procrastination?

Am I even capable?

What if I am doing something wrong?

Yet again I gently remind myself, 'I am the most important task and I am worthy of this rest.'

I don't have answers to the asked and unasked questions.

I also don't have a timeline, as to what is next.

All I know is I need myself in this very moment.

I trust myself to show up when I am ready.

I will not overlook myself for the tasks to be accomplished.

No matter how many times, I will keep reminding myself,

'I am the most important task and worthy of this rest.'

Close or Far

Am I moving close to be healed or moving far from it - adding more wounds?

Why healing is not a choice? Some of us might be just ok living the half-hearted but somewhat stable life. We don't choose healing, it chooses us, and when it does, there is no looking back.

You can't leave the process halfway, you can't quit in the middle.

I have been on this journey like a dedicated student, feeling every dark emotion that comes with it, I am shattered from within, in pieces.

Still, I don't see the light; the books and teachers have been telling about.

I don't know if I am even moving in the right direction.

I wish I could say I can't do this anymore….

Wrong, I say this ten times a day. I wish someone listens

and say, 'She was not ready for this transformation, let's leave her.'

As a human I have my limitations, and who better than you, who has created me to understand this. As if living with anxiety and depression was not enough, we add childhood trauma, physical pain, health fear to it.

How am I supposed to walk, when I can barely crawl?

How I wish most of the days, that I just vanish into thin air or melt into mother earth and it all ends.

I have been living in my head and not in this world for past so many years.

Is surviving just enough ?

Can't be.

We need to do our Karma.

And my Karma can't be just surviving, not collapsing every day.

Something in me just knows there is more, that I can do, I want to do and I will do.

Is this my faith in myself or The Universe's faith in me ?

I don't know, and its not important to know

What is important is to realise how beautifully the Universe holds me, protects me and guides me through my journey.

The Journey of coming far yet so close.

Struggles

Struggles are part of life.

We struggle more when we try and resist.

If we take a pause and think, what are we resisting?

The struggle?

No, we are already in it. Aren't we?

We are resisting the change that will come with it.

We fear it because that is new, we have not seen it.

If instead of resisting we just be, the struggle will pass, and we will evolve, that's the change.

The Noise

Feeling the silence amidst chaos.

Fighting the noise amidst absolute silence.

I have been in both these places.

Been there many times, still difficult to predict which place I land.

Sometimes wanting to get lost in the crowd like no one sees you.

Sometimes wanting to be rescued even when I am alone.

I have been in both these places….

Honouring my free-flowing tears for they are my emotions.

Hiding them and sobbing alone to not be seen as weak.

I have been in both these places…

Really wanting to be one of the two, to be ok with being both.

I have come a long way,

From trying to hold the waters with all my might,

To floating freely with its current.

I have come a long way.

From fearing to losing everything

To accept everything is temporary

I have come a long way.

From getting tired of doing things to make me loved

To loving myself for who I am

I have come a long way.

From being right and the bigger one to forgive people

To forgiving because I deserve freedom

I have come a long way.

From begging to save me from pain

To asking for strength to go through it with grace

I have come a long way.

From wanting to know all answers and completing my story

In Search: Becoming who you are...

To accepting questions with no answers

I have come a long way.

From craving deeply to hear, 'You are brave and I am so proud of you'

To telling my six-year-old self – 'I am proud of you.'

I have come a long way.

From seeing life as binary, to knowing life happens somewhere in between

I have come a long way.

It takes a while before we realise, we are the source and we are the destination. The journey is what we have to complete.

The realisation makes us see we were always complete; we were finding something that was only to be felt, within us.

Life is neither a punishment, nor a revenge, it's an opportunity to come back home to ourselves.

Frames

Frames, these Frames.

Who built these? Is it the society, or family or is it me?

The frames, the one with rough and sharp edges

The frames, which hurt every time I try and fit in.

I have tried my best to fit in, I swear I have, every time letting go a little bit of myself outside the frame.

What the world sees is the 'Me' inside the frame, I ache for the parts left behind.

The pain that comes with it is difficult to understand and resolve. The focus always remains on easing the pain, sometimes with the applauds that comes being the beautiful frame I am, sometimes the validation that 'I am enough and loved'.

Whatever I try, the pain never goes away fully, with each passing year and every milestone that I achieve, with person I add to my list, the grip gets stronger.

Why am I choosing the pain? Why have I born it all along?

It's me who tried walking into the frame, it has to be me walking out of it too.

When did this simple understanding became so complicated?

If the frame was for me, I would have been made that way.

'Walk out of the frame - the box that tries to limit you.

Take your entire self with you and embrace it. Experience life, choose freedom over pain.'

My Story

I was the victim in my story. I faced a lot in this journey, which I don't know why?

Why did no one ever think about me? Why was I left behind? Why was I not loved? Why was I not protected?

I wanted to be seen, to be held and loved, all my life.

I wanted people to acknowledge my pain and to be loved. I wanted this so badly, even at the cost of sympathy, toxic relationships and myself.

I continued to get hurt and abandoned; I continued to overlook myself for others.

All this made me very strong, strong enough to take care of myself.

Strong enough that I needed no one. I fought with all the demons and stood strong, my expectations from the world ceased to exist.

I was not vulnerable, I didn't crave for attention, love or security.

I am a HERO in my story now - the warrior who rises against all odds.

Now I am critical, judging everyone for what they can't do. What I could achieve and they have not, yet.

I am at a position where I can judge people, for I have come this far.

As a victim I was lonely, I am lonely as a Hero too.

What is this happening?

I am still waiting to be loved and be joyful.

What went wrong? Why am I not rewarded for being a Hero, not giving up.

I finally understand.

I am neither a victim nor a hero in my story. I am the writer and this is my story. I choose to respond to situations with my best understanding.

Others make a choice too - some with and some without realisation

I focus to write my story and not evaluate other stories.

'We are not jury here for other's stories, we are writer of our own stories.'

In Search: Becoming who you are...

'When Storm strikes, strongest is not the house that survives but the one that rebuilds.'

Acknowledgements

'Life is a continuous learning and evolution journey.

While being in this journey we often don't realise what significant role some people play in shaping it.

Big or small, consciously, or unconsciously, one time or always - there is someone who shows up in a special way.

That rough road that we all have travelled - there is someone who walks that with us.

That intersection, where we must take a decision and feel confused, there is someone partnering with us to find the right path.

That dark hour where we feel lost and scared, there is someone showing us the light of hope and love.'

To all those who heard me, saw me fall, loved me the way I am, who celebrated with me and saw me cry - A big thank you to my family and circle of friends.

I have many people to thank for this creation – first and

foremost my guarding angels for choosing me, trusting me, and looking after me.

Sagar Azad and team, Anectode Publishing House, for showing faith and publishing my work.

Rohit for patiently partnering in my journey, for never giving up on me.

Naina for always inspiring me and being my biggest cheerleader.

My teachers and therapists- Gaurav Arora, Col. Sudip Mukerjee, Poonam Jalan, Coach Nizam, Surbhee Singh, who showed me the light and gave me strength to go on. I am a good student because of you.